WEYK GLOBAL
BOOK SERIES

ZACHARY LUKASIEWICZ

WEYK GLOBAL MEDIA
Lincoln, Nebraska
www.weykglobal.com

Related Courses & Workshops: WeykGlobal.com
LinkedIn: linkedin.com/in/zdrake2013
More about the author: weykglobal.com/leadership
Please send errors, comments, and speaking inquiries to
hey@weykglobal.com

The goal in releasing this book series is to help narrow the gap between professional marketers and industry newcomers. The idea here is to provide necessary information to passionate individuals to make their business dreams a reality. Our marketing materials - including our courses and workshops - are all aligned on this front.

For Whom Is This Book Intended?

This book is meant for start-ups and small businesses that lack marketing-savvy staff but have a need to intelligently expand the reach of their goods or services. These companies may not have the budget to hire external marketing help, and may also find traditional Google tools to be intimidating. We seek to educate and demystify the online marketplace for these organizations.

What Does It Do?

Using a series of lessons, case studies, and quizzes (if you opt for our online courses), this book and its entire series guides you through 3-5 minute story-based chapters on search marketing, content marketing, PR & Media and more. All in all, we cover eighteen different topics. Depending on your sense of humor, our case studies can cause a few chuckles as you think about, for example, how Connor the karaoke rental equipment guy should improve his search results.

The lessons in this book are heavy on strategy and light on execution. Though this book helps readers differentiate between marketing tactics and identify the best strategies for different businesses, it does not go so far as to provide a detailed walk-through of execution using Google tools. That said, it certainly provides enough information to begin taking steps in the right direction.

How Does It Do It?

This book handles dry topics well, making consistency paramount. This keeps readers engaged in the lessons, with no time to lose focus.

Not only highly interactive, the chapters are also very brief at 3-5 minutes. There are also notes about various courses and workshops to help reinforce the takeaways.

Recommending This Book

Reviewing all of the chapters takes less than 45 minutes. As a digital marketing instructor for Growth(X) Academy, I integrate these essentials into my lessons on search marketing and content marketing in order to reinforce concepts.

FIRST BUILD AN AUDIENCE, THEN MAKE PRODUCTS

- Why should I work on building an audience before making my product?
- How do I use content marketing to build an audience?
- How do I use my audience to figure out which products to sell?

Johan and Alberta are two fashion model friends who like to play tennis when they're not walking the runway.

Johan and Alberta love everything about the sport – except the clothes. After a match, they start talking about how boring they think tennis fashion is. This gives them a big idea: They could make and sell their own line of vogue tennis apparel.

Johan and Alberta know style, but they've never started a business or made a product and they're not sure if there's a market for more fashionable tennis clothing.
Let's help them find out.

Usually a business creates a product, then markets it to their target audience. But there's also an "audience first" approach to making products.

In the "audience first" model, you still need to identify and research a target audience. But then, instead of creating a product, you engage with that audience through content marketing like social media and blog posts.

As you create unique content and work to build an online community around it, you can research and learn more about which products and services your audience really wants.

You can then create a new product based on these insights. Then, when you're ready to launch your product, you have the big advantage of already having a loyal audience that's familiar with your brand.

LISTEN UP
Your first step is to think about who's in your target audience. What type of people are they? Where are they active online? What are their main interests? Which of those interests is your brand looking to cater to?

Instead of developing products for the target audience you've found, create and curate online content that they'll enjoy.

For Johan and Alberta, this could mean starting a tennis style blog that will attract the most fashion-conscious players.

Content can be videos, images, or written posts. To keep people coming back, you'll need to post consistently. It often helps to create a schedule of what and when you'll publish to keep you organized and on track.

After you start making and sharing content, pay close attention to which posts are popular and unpopular so you can craft your future content to appeal to what your audience likes most.

TIP
Learn more about your audience by asking questions. Johan and Alberta could ask readers about their favorite tennis accessory, and the responses could reveal something about their audience, like maybe people are really into patterned headbands.

Once you're making content, you can run social media ads to promote it and grow your audience.

Social media channels provide tools that allow you to target specific demographics and those who show interest in subjects and types of content that are similar to yours.

You can also look into collaborating with other sites that serve your target audience. For example, Johan and Alberta could write guest posts about fashion on general tennis sites and link back to their fashion blog.

TIP
Collect people's emails by including calls to action (CTAs) in your posts. Encourage people to sign up for a newsletter or email alerts by selling the value of your special offers and exclusive information. Then, when you launch a product, you have a jumpstart on your email marketing.

When you have an audience, think of new product ideas that could meet their needs and wants. Then share these ideas and see how people respond.

Johan and Alberta could create shirt designs, post images on their blog, and ask readers which ones they like. When their audience shows interest in a design, Johan and Alberta know that's a good one to make and sell.

If your audience expresses that they want a certain product, consider offering it via pre-order. This helps your potential customers become actual customers, and helps you get the revenue you might need to make your product.

Tell your readers how many products you're making and keep them informed about how many are left. This helps encourage them to buy while supplies last. Then repeat the process with other product ideas.

Just remember to keep producing content while working to sell products. This will allow you to continue building your audience and making more and more sales.

DO THIS NOW

Building an audience can seem like a long process at first, so let's get started by making a list of to-do's you can work on now.

If you're participating in the course, go to the next section to access your self assessment.

KEY TAKEAWAYS

1. Building an audience first allows you to research and test which potential products people want most.
2. Consistently creating and curating relevant videos, images, and written posts about topics will help attract readers and hopefully build a community.
3. Once you've built an audience, ask for direct feedback about which products they want and need.

MOVE PAST FAILURE WITH EFFECTIVE STORYTELLING

- Why is it important that my brand acknowledges its failures?
- How should I tell the story of a failure?
- How can I show that I've moved past a failure?

Imagine there's an online pet food store called Kimble's Kibbles that touts its products as superfood for cats and dogs.

Thanks to positive reviews from 2- and 4-legged customers alike, business is booming and the Kimble's team is working overtime as new sales continue to pour in. Everything's going great.

Now imagine Kimble's Kibbles fills hundreds of dog food orders with bags of cat food. Whoops. With hungry pups on their hands, unhappy customers start barking about the mix-up on social media. How should Kimble's respond?

Making the occasional blunder is just part of doing business. So why should you invest time in crafting a narrative of your failure?

In today's interconnected, social media-driven world, there's no hiding from failure. Word is going to get out. But telling a compelling story about your mistake can help prevent it from turning into an all-out disaster.

When something goes wrong, you need to be able to talk about your failure honestly and specifically, without making excuses.

If you ignore or downplay what the public knows to be true, you may come across as dishonest and tone deaf. This can undo the hard work you've done to build the popularity of your brand and your products among your target audience.

No one wants to buy dog food – or anything else – from a dishonest company. Mishandling failure and appearing insincere or evasive can give your competitors an advantage and an opportunity to snatch away your business.

When you choose to talk about failure in a smart and thoughtful way, you come across as accountable and self-aware. This can limit the damage to your brand and go a long way towards retaining customers.

LISTEN UP

Talking about your mistakes doesn't mean painting your business as a failure. Instead, redefine failure as an unsuccessful outcome. It isn't the end of the story, but it is a part that needs to be acknowledged.

The first step to telling the story of a failure is to choose your words carefully.

Words like "because" and "why" make it sound like you're trying to explain things away. It's better to stick to the facts and summarize the sequence of events. Tell the story of how you failed, not why.

For example, Kimble's Kibbles can take responsibility for their failure by saying: "We mislabeled our Feline's Feast cat food and sent incorrect orders to hundreds of our customers."

This is likely to go over a lot better than saying: "Because of a labelling error, some of our customers received incorrect orders."

Your failure affected customers, but it affected you too. Describing emotions and reactions will make you relatable and prove that you care.

Showing emotions can be more effective than just telling them. You can paint a picture of how you and your employees were affected by describing the actual sequence of events.

Kimble's could say: "When we learned that we'd sent the wrong products to customers, the whole Kimble's team was distraught, and we all gathered on the factory floor to see what had gone wrong."

This is better than just saying: "The whole Kimble's team was distraught when it turned out our orders were mixed up."

The last step to telling the story of a failure is to talk about how you've fixed the problem and are moving forward.

Discussing how you addressed the root cause of the failure will demonstrate change and improvement. This can help earn your audience's trust and business back.

You don't want to be vague. It's not enough for Kimble's to say: "We have reviewed our shipping processes and taken measures to ensure this won't happen again."

It's better to be specific and say: "To ensure the accuracy of our orders, Kimble's has added additional verification steps to our packaging and shipping processes and established a 24-hour support hotline."

DO THIS NOW
Now that you know how to talk about failure, think about a brand you've recently heard about that experienced a mishap or failure.

If you're participating in the course, go to the next section to access your self assessment.

KEY TAKEAWAYS
1. Acknowledging failure can show that you are account-

ZACHARY LUKASIEWICZ

able and self-aware, limiting the damage to your brand.
2. You should tell the story of a failure honestly and specifically, without making excuses.
3. Describing your reactions and the specific steps you took to fix the problem can help you move past a failure.

GET CUSTOMERS INTERESTED BY TELLING A GREAT STORY

- How can I use my own experiences to help my business?
- What's the personal approach to storytelling?
- What's the higher purpose approach?

Storytelling isn't just for gatherings around the campfire. It's also a way to make people care about your business.

What if you don't have a story all loaded up and ready to tell?

Here's the good news: No business is boring.

You just need to figure out what makes yours so special.

Imagine that there's a business owner named Michael who makes hats for cats, donating part of his proceeds to animal rescues.

What's a better starting point for Michael's story?

There are two ways you can approach your business story: personal or higher purpose.

A personal approach centers on the moment or moments in your life that sparked your business idea.

A higher purpose approach hinges on a greater, shared goal that your business already has.

We'll look at the personal approach first and see how tech company FiLIP uses it.

Founded in 2009, FiLIP makes smart phone watches that keep young children in touch with their parents. But that's not the personal story behind the business.

FiLIP is actually named after the son of the founder, Sten Kirkbak. When Filip (the son) was three, Sten briefly lost him in a crowded mall – which inspired Sten to create FiLIP the company.

He also appeals to moms and dads with photos of him and Filip. This helps people relate personally to FiLIP, instead of seeing it as just technology.

Sten tells this story to customers, starting with his mission statement.

Now let's look at how KIND Healthy Snacks uses the higher purpose approach.

KIND Healthy Snacks' higher purpose is to make the world a little kinder, one act at a time.

Partnering with their community, the company inspires people to do the KIND thing. They call this the KIND Movement.

One part of that movement is KIND Causes. It helps people and organizations bring socially-impactful ideas to life through monthly grants.

They also created STRONG & KIND, an initiative that breaks down cultural stereotypes and proves it's strong to be kind.

REMEMBER
FiLIP started with a personal story and KIND started with a higher purpose...but both are engaging and stand out.

When you create your story, keep this in mind: The best stories are specific, they take people on a journey, and they aren't just about buzzwords and trends.

DO THIS NOW

Business stories can be a mix of personal and higher purpose, but it's easier to use one direction to begin creating your story. Let's figure out which direction might be easier for you. `

If you're participating in the course, go to the next section to access your self assessment.

KEY TAKEAWAYS
1. Every business has an interesting story to tell.
2. You can focus on your personal journey and passion for your business.
3. Don't forget, you can tap into your higher purpose.

HOW A PUNCHLINE CAN SEND A STRONG MESSAGE

- How can I use humor to connect with my audience?
- What techniques can help me add humor to my marketing?
- How do I make sure I'm using humor in the right context?

They say that laughter is the best medicine. As a marketer, it can also be the best way to get your message across to your target audience.

Whether you're launching a campaign or doing a presentation, using humor helps you connect with your audience. That's because laughter lowers people's defenses and makes them more open to new ideas and points of view.

People's brains also register humorous moments as positive memories. So if you present an idea wrapped in humor, people are more likely to remember it.

Let's look at an example. The CMO of a global beauty company is presenting a 105-slide deck about global growth, and wants to add a bit of humor to it. How can she make her slide about global sales of the hottest new lipstick more memorable?

Let's see how Hotels.com used humor to differentiate themselves from their competitors.

Hotels.com wanted to stand out in a competitive online booking industry. They decided to humorously play on their name, implying that it made them the obvious choice for booking hotels.

As part of a North American ad campaign that has since gone global, they created Captain Obvious, a superfan.

Captain Obvious' humor came from him pointing out things that are wildly apparent, like, "Hotel gym is short for gymnasium!"

The ad campaign's humor rested in the combination of the situational humor, the quirky appearance of the character, and his deadpan delivery of extremely obvious facts.

This humorous approach reinforced the connection between hotel bookings and Hotels.com in the target audience's minds. The campaign was a hit, resulting in a 30% increase in site traffic to Hotels.com.

LISTEN UP
Humor isn't just for ad campaigns.

It's also a great storytelling device you can use in all your marketing, like social media content or blog posts, to engage any audience.

The first step to creating a humorous story is finding the game. This is coming up with a funny element in the story you want to tell in your marketing campaign.

Do this by creating a main character with an unusual trait. For example, imagine a horse rescue shelter is creating a social campaign around "horse success stories." One features Helen – a bookish, globetrotting horse.

Once you find the game, ask yourself: "If this funny/unusual thing is true, what else is true in this world?" This will help you discover humorous elements without resorting to cheap gags.

Next, bring the game to life by setting a vivid scene and describing how the character moves and talks.

After you've established the scene, heighten the game by pushing the character and situation to the limit.

For example, Helen embarks on a journey of self-discovery spanning from Paris to India. She recounts her journey in an online diary called "Eat, Neigh, Love."

It is important to keep humor consistent by obeying the rules of the game. Every story has its own internal logic. Maintaining these rules, however arbitrary or absurd, will allow you to go as big as you want.

TIP
Think of your marketing message like a punchline. You want to build the story over time so that the final message will stand out.

Humor is all about context, especially when used in marketing. A joke is only funny when told at the right place, at the right time, to the right audience.

Make sure the humor is timely and relatable to your target audience. Jokes about politics can be funny...unless they're about an election 10 years ago or your target audience isn't of voting age.

Humor is the # 1 characteristic associated with high view rates for ads, but make sure the humor you use is right for the medium: A joke that works in a 30-second TV ad might not work in a print ad.

DO THIS NOW
Now that you've seen how humor can help you connect with your audience, let's see how and where you can apply humor in your marketing.

If you're participating in the course, go to the next section to access your self assessment.

KEY TAKEAWAYS
    1. Humor is an effective device for helping to connect

with your audience.

2. Think of your marketing message like a punchline, and build your humorous story over time.

3. Even though humor it's a great way to engage with your audience, make sure it's used in the right context and situation.

FIND A TARGET AUDIENCE THAT'S NOT GENERIC

- Why should I avoid generic descriptions of my target audience?
- What's a good way to define my target audience?
- How does this help me stand out from my competitors?

Soccer moms. Yuppies. Tweens. You might hear businesses using labels like these when they talk about target audiences.

It helps them narrow their ideal customers down into an easy group to market to. It makes sense...in theory.

But can a generic target audience like soccer moms really help you do the best marketing?

When it comes to target audiences, remember this: Customers are people, not stereotypes.

Really understanding your customer means knowing more about them than just their sex, age group, social status, and what type of job they have.

What you really need to know is WHY. As in: Why they act, think, and lead their lives the way they do.

Basically, you need to know your target audience as well as you know your closest friend.

You may be thinking, "Broad stereotypes are easier to come up with. Why can't I market to 30-something hipster dads?"

Here's why: It's difficult – if not impossible – to be everything to everyone. There's just too many competitors out there, and you won't distinguish yourself from them.

And stereotypes can lead you to assume your target audience is one group when it's actually a completely different group altogether.

How do you avoid the broad stereotype trap? Think about the major assumptions you've made about your customers – and challenge them.

Ask yourself which of these assumptions need to be validated before they can become a truth. Also, list out anything you might not know about your customers that you should explore.

As you whittle away at stereotypes, keeping some Dos and Don'ts in mind will help you find a better target audience.

Target Audience Dos:

DEFINE THEM NARROWLY
Find the nitty gritty details of your audience.

THINK LIKE THEM
See the world (and your business) through their eyes.

GO DEEP
Pay attention to context, mindset, emotions, motivations, and desires.

DO YOUR RESEARCH
Look into your theories and back them up with data.

Target Audience Don'ts:

BE GENERIC
AKA, avoid stereotypes. Look for what makes your audience unique.

RELY ONLY ON DEMOGRAPHICS
Race, gender, and other stats won't help you reach narrow definitions.

MARKET TO "EVERYONE"
The "entire world" is not a good target audience, nor an easy one to reach.

FOLLOW YOUR COMPETITORS
Your target audience is not necessarily the same as your competitors'.

LISTEN UP
What those Dos and Don'ts are really saying is: Look at your audience as three-dimensionally as possible.

You'll find a lot of different ways to do this, but we'll take you through a few jumping off points.

You can look at definitions that are normally considered generic and broad, and then begin paring them down and refining them.

Instead of the very large 18 to 49 year old age group, you can look at specific age ranges like early 20's or early 30's.

Along with age, you can look at where your target audience is: city, suburbs, countryside, another country, etc.

What education level does your target audience have? High school, Bachelor's, Master's, or higher? Or are they self-educated?

Also look at what type of job they have: professional, blue collar, business owner, etc.

These descriptions do a decent job of defining your audience narrowly, but you can go further by looking at lifestyles and emotions.

Look at what they like to do and what type of hobbies they have. Are they into arts, science, socializing, etc.?

Your target audience's values can also tell you a lot about them. Research what they believe in: honesty, hard work, community, family, etc.

Finally, look at how they view your business and product. Do they think of you as a pastime, a necessary evil, an escape, or something else?

Let's see how Pinterest, the visual discovery tool for ideas you can try in real life, found success by narrowing down their target audience.

Founders Ben Silbermann and Evan Sharp originally created Pinterest as a tool to help themselves collect visual inspiration they found online. When they decided to make Pinterest available to others, they at first weren't sure who they should market to.

One conference later, they found traction with a community of lifestyle bloggers, which helped populate Pinterest with great content. Based on this, Ben and Evan could have easily chosen the broad target audience of "creatives."

Instead, Ben and Evan studied how Pinterest's audience was growing organically. They looked at why people were using their tool and how they were using it.

Through this, they discovered new communities of Pinterest fans – like people who weren't professional designers, but who were still interested in easy, creative ideas for home decor, fashion, and cooking.

Pinterest focused its marketing to reach this narrow target audience, which helped them quickly grow their user base and develop a global community of Pinners.

DO THIS NOW
To start defining your target audience like Pinterest, think of one current customer who you really value. Then ask yourself some questions about that person.

If you're participating in the course, go to the next section to access your self assessment.

KEY TAKEAWAYS
1. Using demographics isn't the only way to find your target audience.
2. Think like your customer and consider their emotions, mindset, needs, and wants.
3. Having a narrow target audience helps you reach your customers better and stand out from your competitors.

WEYK GLOBAL LEADERSHIP

Zachary Lukasiewicz is the Managing Director of Weyk Global.

Originally from Omaha, Nebraska and attended Drake University in Des Moines, Iowa. He served as a tri-chair for the Human Capital committee of Capital Crossroads, the 10-year plan for Central Iowa, where he focused on the attraction and retention of Des Moines residents from cradle to career.

Zachary has operated 50+ accelerator assistance programs and in-house workshops, and staffed marketing teams around the globe.

Zachary's focus is marketing investment - sourcing the best talent, recruiting domain experts and executing on his proven playbook and delivering the best possible experience. He sets the strategic direction and client profile within the program, including a curated team of mentors, investors and business advisors.

Zachary is responsible for making the initial relationships. He takes overall ownership of each programs' success and partners with other operations units external to Weyk Global to ensure exceptional delivery of exceptional marketing programs, and is ultimately responsible for turning good companies into great ones.

Additional:

- Builds systems around market research and data-driven management—especially in budget allocation, paid/organic, and navigating complex customer cadences.
- Experience building marketing infrastructure and communication processes throughout US Techstars classes, reducing acquisition costs with greater capacity and cost-effectiveness
- A recognized expert on US social media in real estate, education, and human resources industries
- A leader with proven skills working with innovative teams to build customer consensus and drive buy-in behavior across purpose-driven organizations
- Motivates large organizations and individual personnel to award-winning performance and achievement
- Leadership experience encompasses direct management of 20+ personnel, over $8.5 million in assets/budgets with a record of five enterprise acquisitions and assisting in seven fundraising rounds

Zachary has served as a management consultant with startups backed by White Star Capital, Hoxton Ventures, Bloomberg Beta, Real Ventures, BDC Capital, Chris Anderson. Eduardo Gentil, Jacqueline Novogratz, Mehdi Alhassani, Ana Carolina, Entrepreneur, Obvious Ventures, MIT, Ittleson Foundation, J.M.Kaplan Fund, SC/E, MassCEC, WhiteHouse.gov, ServiceCorps, The One Foundation, The Godley Family Foundation, the Boston Foundation, Boris Jabes, Ilya

Sukhar, Chris DeVore, Alex Payne, DJF, Liquid 2 Ventures, GSF, Sanjay Jain, Felix Anthony, Uma Raghavan, and TiE LaunchPad. Zachary's early experience comes from working under business leaders at market-leading companies including ISoft Data Systems, LukeUSA, AlphaPrep.net, Staffing Nerd, Immun.io, Reflect.io, Validated.co, Shaun White Enterprises, Solstice.us, Swym, Staffing Robot, Hatchlings, Coaching Actuaries, 8 to Great, Target, Paylease, MidAmerican Energy, and R&R Realty Group.

Weyk Global offers two types of in-house training:

- Our workshops at any location:
All advertised courses can be taught in the location of your choice at a time convenient for you. We will ensure the course is specific to your business and sector.

- Our workshops tailored to your needs:
We can design bespoke training to meet the needs of your business. You can provide a brief or we will work with you to develop the training resources to help you achieve your goals.

Analytics Fundamentals

Discover the fundamentals of analytics and the different tools that will help you draw insights from analytics.

In this workshop, we'll examine the fundamentals of analytics, exploring the tools and their most appropriate use. You'll discover how to draw insights from analytics, enabling you to predict emerging trends. This course is designed for those who are curious in nature, enjoy problem-solving and prefer a self- learning, exploratory approach to knowledge.

Career Accelerator

Ensure you have the skills and knowledge to quickly start making an impact in your organization.

Getting into the industry is always challenging; university provides many of the concepts but not necessarily all the skills to be really ready to make a difference. This workshop enables junior marketers to be successful sooner, by understanding the basic concepts and platforms of their day-to-day jobs and getting the skills they need to become more effective in their roles.

Content Marketing Strategy

Examine all areas of content marketing and the role they play in digital, marketing and business strategies.

Best-practice case studies will walk you through all the components of an effective content strategy. You'll also focus on how to create, distribute and manage your content.

Consumers prefer to be engages with a brand via a story or conversation, so the power of content is immeasurable. Through both in-class discussion and practical exercises, we'll explore how consumer behavior fuels this power and how you can develop your content marketing strategy to be just as powerful. You'll also learn how to properly measure its effectiveness.

Conversion Rate Optimization

Harness the power of conversion and learn how to optimize your site to achieve your online objectives.

This powerful workshop will teach you the fundamentals of how to turn your hard-earned website visitors into leads and sales. Applying the insights you'll get will help you improve your conversion rates leading to increased online revenue and lead generation. If you want to know more about the fast-growing marketing discipline of conversion rate optimization, this is the best workshop for you to dip your toe in the water and get started.

Copywriting (Advanced)

Explore new, clever and engaging ways to push your writing to the next level.

Writing today is an indispensable skill and if you want to excel, you need more than just the basics. Throughout this workshop, you'll engage with and produce strategic and compelling copy that will attract readers.

Copywriting (Essentials)

Discover the essential techniques for writing effective copy.

One of our most popular workshops, copywriting essentials explores the structure, rules and techniques in copywriting. Learn to craft compelling headlines, structure documents and most importantly, engage your reader.

Copywriting for Content Marketing

Plan, write and publish creative content that engages readers and keeps them coming back for more.

During this course, you'll explore copywriting for blogs, PR, social media posts and articles. Discover new techniques and master traditional ones. Explore a variety of effective, compelling and fresh techniques for copywriting for content marketing during this hands-on workshop.

Creative Leadership

Develop senior creative leadership skills to improve business effectiveness.

Winning the promotion and becoming a senior manager

doesn't mean you are ready for all that is ahead of you as you take on more responsibility and manage a team or sets of teams. Becoming a good leader in the new digital economy is not an easy task as there are many opportunities and challenges to tackle every single day. This course will help develop a creative culture, nurture creative talent, help build trusted business relationships that allow you and others to succeed and link business and creative needs with technology and innovation.

Customer Journey Mapping

Ensure customer understanding is at the heart of your marketing.

Create a compelling experience for customers using analytics tools and insights. Customer insights are a crucial part of any marketing strategy or campaign, and yet most marketing strategies are developed with a focus on the product attributes or benefits we want to communicate. In this course, you'll discover the fundamentals of analytics and the different tools that will help you draw insights from data to create a compelling customer experience.

CX for CMOs

This workshop brings together all the critical pieces you need to know in the age of information excess.

CX is not one thing, it's every way the customer experiences your brand and business. This workshop, curated by CMOs, brings together all of the critical pieces that are demanded of CMOs today in delivering customer experience - the holy grail of marketing – giving you real clarity on how to apply these insights to your business.

Data Analytics for Marketers

Engage with data analysis and discover how it can deliver

marketing effectiveness.

This short workshop will help you make sense of the high volume and increasingly complex data available to marketers, as well as build a high-level view of the tools, techniques and processes you might use in the process.

Data Driven Marketing Leadership

Broaden your skill set as a leader and develop a data-driven marketing mindset to support your technical team leaders.

During this workshop, you'll be provided with an outline of how business operations and governance work within the field of data, how to lead and inspire your technical teams and to provide cross-functional management and integration.

Data Driven Marketing Practitioner

Learn how to use data to drive your business forward.

In this workshop, we'll show you how to access both primary and third-party data, develop actionable insights, explore data research and perform analytical techniques. This will help you to tell stories with data, benchmark insights from analytics and incorporate the latest solutions and models to tackle business problems. Our Data-driven Practitioner Workshop is designed for those who have access to data directly and/or who have a team and prefer a self-learning, exploratory approach to learning.

Data Driven Marketing Strategy

Discover how a data-driven marketing strategy can deliver a successful customer-centric marketing presence.

In this workshop, we examine a more strategic approach to using your data. This allows us to uncover information about how customers interact with your brand and identify areas that would otherwise go undetected.

Data Visualization

Establish your own visualization techniques that will help sell your analytics results to business decision makers.

In this workshop, you'll learn how to translate and present analytics in an enticing manner. You'll draw upon insights from data and convert these into commercial insights. This workshop is designed for those who are curious in nature, enjoy problem-solving and prefer a self-learning, exploratory approach to knowledge.

Digital Analytics for Marketers

Introducing an accessible approach to measuring, analyzing and optimizing digital marketing activity.

Learn to apply proven marketing theories to real world examples. Unlock the power of data to enhance decision making and campaign planning. This workshop has been designed so a difficult topic is now simple, straightforward and easy to grasp.

Digital Copywriting Essentials

Discover the essential skills and practices for writing effective digital copy.

Whether it's a quick status update or detailed blog post, writing on a digital platform is already a part of your day. The structures and styles for online are, however, different - there is no one-size-fits-all approach to different platforms. For your copy to cut through the current cluttered digital environment, it needs to be engaging. Through tested techniques, you'll discover the art of writing engaging digital copy for search purposes, emails, websites and social media.

Digital Marketing Campaign Planning & Management

Broaden your skills base by discovering how digital can make your campaigns thrive.

During this workshop, you'll explore the practical elements of digital marketing and how you can integrate them within your brand's activity. You'll learn to determine the right resources, budget, plan and identify opportunities for optimization.

Digital Marketing Channels

Discover how each digital marketing channel can deliver you a customer-centric marketing presence.

In this workshop, we examine each channel individually and uncover information about channel contributions to the consumer journey and how to utilize it in your marketing activity.

Digital Marketing Essentials

Discover industry tips and tricks for successfully incorporating digital channels into your campaigns.

In this two-day intensive workshop, you'll explore the foundations of each digital channel, how they work and how they can fit together to deliver on your marketing objectives. We'll also look at digital tactics, strategies and processes and how you can tie them all together in an effective way.

Digital Marketing Foundations

Broaden your skill set and develop a foundational knowledge of the digital landscape, data, content and customer experience.

During this workshop you'll be provided with an outline of the core foundations and principles of digital marketing. Explore the role of data and content and how this can shape customer experience.

Digital Marketing Strategy

Uncover a framework for successful digital marketing.

Whether it's your business, industry, or campaign, digital continues to have a significant impact on the way we operate. During this workshop, you'll be provided with a framework for crafting a digital marketing strategy. To get the most out of this two-day intensive workshop, you should have a good understanding of the basic digital marketing tactics.

Email Marketing

Boost your email marketing results with proven techniques, technical and strategy improvements.

Explore new ways of using email marketing in your overall communications strategy and learn how to deploy marketing automation techniques to drive customer engagement.

Practical Predictive Analytics

Develop a deeper understanding of predictive analytics.

Using predictive analytics, discover how you can forecast, model and optimize data to create opportunities and prevent loss. To get the most out of this course, you should have a solid knowledge of analytics and have ideally spent some time working in the field - over three years' experience is recommended.

Privacy & Marketing Compliance

A commercial approach to compliance for data-driven marketers and advertisers.

Learn how to protect and enhance your brand's reputation by ensuring your marketing and advertising meets customer expectations and complies with the privacy and marketing content laws.

Programmatic Advertising

Adopt a simple, fresh and effective platform to power your marketing.

Programmatic advertising is reshaping the digital landscape as it's automating everything. Marketers need to exploit the power of automated media trading and learn how they can optimize its productivity. In this workshop, we'll explore various programmatic models and the different technologies available for implementation.

Retention & Loyalty Marketing Strategy

Discover the four pillars to building a comprehensive customer retention and loyalty marketing strategy.

In this two-day intensive workshop, you'll adopt a framework for retaining customers through loyalty marketing strategies. We'll explore the power behind loyalty and advocacy initiatives in both traditional and digital techniques. The proven effectiveness of keeping a customer and nurturing their loyalty and advocacy is where the value is derived.

SEM Essentials

Simple yet successful ways to enhance your search results.

Paid search can transform your business without a huge spend. It's a cost effective, highly convenient channel. See how it can strengthen your search engine marketing, morph into a wider digital strategy for your business and leverage other channels.

Sentiment Analysis

Discover best-practice approaches that use modern text mining and predictive analytics techniques to gain insight into consumer opinions and forecast behaviors.

In this course, you'll advance your knowledge of sentiment and content analysis, and opinion mining, develop a deeper understanding of how to work with unstructured text data (in particular, data retrieved from social media) and learn how traditional machine learning/predictive analytics techniques can be used for the purposes of sentiment analysis. It is recommended that you complete the Practical Predictive Analytics Workshop prior to taking this workshop. This workshop is designed for those who are curious in nature, enjoy problem solving and prefer a self-learning, exploratory approach to knowledge.

SEO Essentials

Find out how SEO drives new customers and better customer engagement.

Score page rankings, better click-throughs, utilize research tools and foster great external links with an effective SEO strategy. Discover what simple techniques can do when applied to your website structure.

Social Media Marketing Essentials

Discover the foundations behind social media marketing and how you can adopt the practices into your own communications mix.

Get up to speed with the latest trends, techniques and technologies in social media and learn to craft your own social media campaign through planning, execution and optimization.

Social Media Marketing Strategy

Research, plan and implement a successful social media marketing strategy from the ground up.

Most organizations and brands are on social media - and if they're not, they should be. Social media is a way for consumers to engage and communicate with brands. But this doesn't mean businesses should just start a Facebook page or Twitter account. It's not that simple, as there are right and wrong strategies to use with each channel. Looking at these channels and their tactics, you'll learn how to develop, implement and measure social media activity.

Community & Customer Relationship Management

- Do you need help improving the efficiency and effectiveness of your marketing management?
- Do you have sufficient time and resources to create and distribute resources to your industry and customer base?
- Are your outreach efforts stagnant or causing disruptions to operations?
- Do you have a potential conflict of interest by handling your ongoing marketing programs with operational resources?

Global Help Desk & Support

- Do you support customers globally, but lack in-house bandwidth and expertise?
- Do you struggle to quantify the value of your marketing program?
- Are you tired of getting blamed for missed opportunities or slow response times?
- Do you have trouble tracking, prioritizing and resolving requests for support?

Marketing Automation Enablement

- Having trouble identifying or selecting marketing automation solutions?
- Do you want more out of your current go-to-market solution?
- Are you in need of consistent communication with your customers?
- Do you lack the budget for technology, but wish you could leverage technology without a capital investment?

Pre-Post M&A Support: Marketing Bridge

- Are you involved in the pre-acquisition due diligence process and concerned with successor liability?
- Do you lack bandwidth or expertise to integrate, oversee or transition a newly acquired company into your marketing program?
- Are you struggling to address customer acquisition risks identified during due diligence?

Agency of Record

- Do you want to grow your marketing team, but lack the budget?
- Do you wish you could leverage the best in industry digital marketing talent without sacrificing equity?
- Are you looking to create a narrative for potential business expansion?
- Do you want access to modular marketing growth without committing to multi-year contracts?

Opportunity Identification & Innovation Management

- Do you need help analyzing the potential savings and benefits from potential customer or product line expansion?
- Do you wish you had time to qualify marketing tools or implement a baseline for business growth?
- Do you have a go-to-marketing plan in place, but lack the staff to manage your day-to-day?

Third Party Vendor Management

- Do you lack the time or resources to audit and ensure your marketing vendors' quality and service performance level?
- Are you tired of correcting errors or performing your vendors' responsibilities?
- Are you unknowingly putting your Company's reputation and compliance at risk by relying on incorrect best practices and roadmap?
- When was the last time you audited your vendor's fees or timeliness of deliveries?

Marketing Program Optimization

- When was the last time you assessed your Company's marketing-related risks, gaps, and challenges?
- Do your processes and procedures reflect your current business requirements and risk tolerance?
- Is your staff configured to support a major marketing migration